NORTHWEST FOREST PLAN
THE FIRST TEN YEARS (1994–2003)

Socioeconomic Monitoring Results
Volume IV: Collaboration

Ellen M. Donoghue, Claudia Stuart, and Susan Charnley

General Technical Report
PNW-GTR-649 Vol. IV
April 2006

 United States
Department of
Agriculture

 Forest
Service

 Pacific Northwest
Research Station

Authors

Ellen M. Donoghue and **Susan Charnley** are research social scientists, U.S. Department of Agriculture, Forest Service, Pacific Northwest Research Station, P.O. Box 3890, Portland, OR 97208; **Claudia Stuart** is a community planner, U.S. Department of Agriculture, Forest Service, Mendocino National Forest, Genetic Resource Center, 2741 Cramer Lane, Chico, CA 95928.

Socioeconomic Monitoring Results
Volume IV: Collaboration

Ellen M. Donoghue, Claudia Stuart, and Susan Charnley

Northwest Forest Plan—The First 10 Years (1994–2003): Socioeconomic Monitoring Results

Susan Charnley, Technical Coordinator

U.S. Department of Agriculture, Forest Service
Pacific Northwest Research Station
Portland, Oregon
General Technical Report PNW-GTR-649 Vol. IV
April 2006

Abstract

Donoghue, Ellen M.; Stuart, Claudia; Charnley, Susan. 2006. Socioeconomic monitoring results. Vol. IV. Collaboration. In: Charnley, S., tech. coord. Northwest Forest Plan—the first 10 years (1994–2003): socioeconomic monitoring results. Gen. Tech. Rep. PNW-GTR-649. Portland, OR: U.S. Department of Agriculture, Forest Service, Pacific Northwest Research Station. 23 p.

One of the Northwest Forest Plan (the Plan) socioeconomic goals was to promote inter-agency collaboration and agency-citizen collaboration in forest management. This volume focuses on agency-citizen collaboration under the Plan. Two formal institutions were set up to promote agency-citizen collaboration in forest management: provincial advisory committees (PACs) and adaptive management areas (AMAs). Chapter 1 synthesizes the literature describing the management and effectiveness of AMAs and PACs during the first decade of the Plan. Chapter 2 examines how collaborative relations and collaboration in forest stewardship evolved on four case-study Forest Service (FS) and Bureau of Land Management (BLM) units and 12 associated communities since the Plan was implemented.

The literature shows that in their first decade, most AMAs failed to meet the Plan's expectations for collaboration. The PACs have been more successful in engaging local communities. The PACs have provided a forum for ongoing, multiparty discussion of forest management issues among decisionmakers and local stakeholders. They have also been successful in completing regionwide, multiparty compliance monitoring. The Plan had direct and indirect, positive and negative, effects on collaborative forest stewardship on the case-study forests and communities.

Keywords: Northwest Forest Plan, socioeconomic monitoring, collaboration, joint forest stewardship, adaptive management areas, provincial advisory committees.

Preface

This report is one of a set of reports produced on this 10-year anniversary of the Northwest Forest Plan (the Plan). The collection of reports attempts to answer questions about the effectiveness of the Plan based on new monitoring and research results. The set includes a series of status and trends reports, a synthesis of all regional monitoring and research results, a report on interagency information management, and a summary report.

The status and trends reports focus on establishing baselines of information from 1994, when the Plan was approved, and reporting change over the 10-year period. The status and trends series includes reports on late-successional and old-growth forests, northern spotted owl population and habitat, marbled murrelet population and habitat, watershed condition, government-to-government tribal relationships, socioeconomic conditions, and monitoring of project implementation under Plan standards and guidelines.

The synthesis report addresses questions about the effectiveness of the Plan by using the status and trends results and new research. It focuses on the validity of the Plan assumptions, differences between expectations and what actually happened, the certainty of these findings, and finally, considerations for the future. The synthesis report is organized in two parts: Part I—introduction, context, synthesis, and summary—and Part II—socioeconomic implications, older forests, species conservation, the aquatic conservation strategy, and adaptive management and monitoring.

The report on interagency information management identifies issues and recommends solutions for resolving data and mapping problems encountered during the preparation of the set of monitoring reports. Information issues inevitably surface during analyses that require data from multiple agencies covering large geographic areas. The goal of this set of reports is to improve the integration and acquisition of interagency data for the next comprehensive report.

The socioeconomic status and trends report is published in six volumes. Volume I of the report contains key findings. Volume II addresses the evaluation question, Are predictable levels of timber and nontimber resources available and being produced? The focus of Volume III is the evaluation question, Are local communities and economies experiencing positive or negative changes that may be associated with federal forest management? Volume IV (this volume) assesses the Plan goal of promoting agency-citizen collaboration in forest management. Volume V reports on public values regarding federal forest management in the Pacific Northwest. Volume VI provides a history of the Northwest Forest Plan socioeconomic monitoring program and a discussion of potential directions for the program.

Summary

One of the Northwest Forest Plan (the Plan) socioeconomic goals was to promote inter-agency collaboration and agency-citizen collaboration in forest management. This volume focuses on agency-citizen collaboration under the Plan. The monitoring team did not monitor interagency coordination and collaboration beacuse resources were not available to do so. Two formal institutions were set up to promote agency-citizen collaboration in forest management: provincial advisory committees (PACs) and adaptive management areas (AMAs). Chapter 1 synthesizes the literature describing the management and effectiveness of AMAs and PACs during the first decade of the Plan. Chapter 2 examines how collaborative relations and collaboration in forest stewardship evolved on four case-study Forest Service (FS) and Bureau of Land Management (BLM) units (the Olympic, Mount Hood, and Klamath National Forests and the Coos Bay BLM District) and 12 associated communities since the Plan was implemented.

The monitoring questions and indicators monitored were the following:

Monitoring questions	Indicators monitored
Chapter 1	
How effective have new forms of collaboration been in engaging local communities?	Summarized the existing literature that describes the management and effectiveness of AMAs and PACs.
How much has collaboration with the public contributed to achieving the other objectives of the new collaborative mechanisms, such as effective resource management?	
How effective have the new forms of collaboration been in providing socio-economic benefits to local communities?	
Chapter 2	
Did agency and citizen collaboration in forest stewardship improve under the Plan, and did relations between local communities and agencies improve?	Level of engagement between community (groups) and agencies
	Types of collaborative forest stewardship activities
	Purpose of collaborations and partnerships
	Benefits of collaboration
	Barriers to collaboration
	Volunteerism

Plan Expectations Regarding Agency-Citizen Collaboration

Some AMAs were expected to be actively managed to contribute to the sustained supply of timber expected under the Plan. Local AMA resource managers and communities were expected to use their combined experience and ingenuity to identify approaches that would achieve the conservation objectives of the Plan, without adhering rigidly to all of its

standards and guidelines. Primary technical objectives were to develop and evaluate monitoring programs and innovative management practices integrating ecological and economic
values. Specific forest management topics to be explored were identified for each AMA.
They ranged in emphasis from intensive timber production to single-species management to
partnerships with state and private land managers.

Adaptive management areas were intended to be prototypes of how forest communities
might be sustained. Land management and regulatory agencies were expected to collaborate
with other government entities, nongovernmental organizations, local groups, landowners,
communities, and citizens to achieve these goals.

Under the record of decision (ROD), PACs were to "provide or coordinate analyses at
the province level that can provide the basis for amendments to Forest and District Plans and
will provide monitoring reports for provinces" (USDA and USDI 1994: E-17). The ROD also
directs that PACs are to "encourage and facilitate information exchange and complementary
ecosystem management among federal and non-federal partners."

Collaborative processes, broadly speaking, were expected to create new ways to involve
local governments, tribes, and the public in managing the region's forests, in addition to
increasing interagency and intergovernmental coordination (Tuchmann et al. 1996). Interagency cooperation and public participation would reduce conflict over forest management
(Tuchmann et al. 1996). The Plan did not have specific expectations related to on-the-ground
collaborative forest stewardship activities outside of adaptive management areas.

Monitoring Results

Although neither AMAs nor PACs have been entirely successful in meeting Plan expectations, both mechanisms have offered significant improvements upon the gridlock and
limited collaborative opportunities available in the early 1990s.

Initial AMA collaboration with local communities showed promise. Early in the period,
the Federal Advisory Committee Act (FACA) chartering process forced federal participants
to temporarily withdraw. Internal agency issues further impaired the ability of AMA managers to collaborate meaningfully. Given these failures, the collaborative synergy envisioned
in the ROD did not materialize. Coordination with the public was not sufficient to leverage
the land management agencies' limited willingness and ability to experiment. Few AMAs
appear to have gone beyond "business as usual" under the land allocations and standards
imposed by the Plan. Accordingly, AMAs have provided little socioeconomic benefit to
local communities beyond the other provisions in the Plan.

The PACs have been more successful in engaging local communities. The PACs have
provided a forum for ongoing, multiparty discussion of forest management issues among
decisionmakers and local stakeholders. In this sense they represent an important step forward over project "scoping" as defined under the National Environmental Policy Act. They
also have been successful in completing regionwide, multiparty compliance monitoring. In
this capacity the Plan's PACs can serve as a basis for future efforts. Although PACs have
served to improve the flow of information and learning among province interest groups,
they have not significantly shaped decisionmaking, and have accordingly been unable to

affect the flow of benefits to local communities. Despite these failings, PACs represent an important interim step toward developing new mechanisms for collaboration.

The Plan has had direct and indirect, positive and negative effects on collaborative forest stewardship on the case-study forests and communities. The Plan's ecosystem focus and emphasis on interagency collaboration has encouraged interactions among public and private landowners and broadened the range of stakeholders and opportunities for collaboration. A variety of groups, together with forest agencies, are pooling time, labor, finances, and ideas to achieve mutually held forest stewardship objectives. Faced with decreased budgets and staffs, the forests have been able to maintain viable, productive, and multi-beneficial collaborative projects and programs. The volunteer programs are good examples of programs that are evolving and seeking new collaborative opportunities in the face of administrative and budgetary constraints.

Lower harvest rates and the resulting lower budgets and staff, which have both direct and indirect ties to the Plan, have influenced trends in collaboration in two key, yet paradoxical ways. With decreasing human and financial resources for forest management activities, the forests have expanded and developed partnerships with groups that share similar resource management goals. The paradox is that, as budget declines serve as an incentive for innovation and expansion of collaboration, they simultaneously constrain and potentially jeopardize collaborative efforts. Agency interviewees expressed concern that reducing staff and resources has made managing collaboration more difficult.

Increased diversity and innovation in collaboration, however, have coincided with a decrease in communication and collaboration with a once-prominent forest stakeholder, namely the timber community. The disconnect between timber-based communities and forest management, and the implication it would have for collaborative relations, were unanticipated consequences of the reduction in timber harvests under the Plan. In general, collaborative activities with members of the case-study communities were minimal, with some exceptions, such as tribes. New connections have yet to replace old timber ties in some communities. Interviewees from former timber-based communities tended to feel disassociated from, or unaware of, current forest policies and practices, or had little direct concern with forest management. And yet, some former timber industry employees who remained in their communities felt that their skills, knowledge, and experience in forest management could serve contemporary forest management but were not being used. Other factors that affected the participation of community residents in collaborative resource management, beyond the necessity of a shared mutual interest or stake, included a shortage of residents with skills to do the work or the time to participate, a lack of consistent players and participation, the local presence—or absence—of organized groups with resources, and the need to struggle to make ends meet.

Contents

Chapter 1: Federal Collaborative Efforts

Claudia Stuart

The Northwest Forest Plan (the Plan) called for federal agencies to coordinate and collaborate with one another in managing federal forests in the Pacific Northwest (Tuchmann et al. 1996: 6, 44–48). It also called for greater collaboration in forest management between agencies and citizens (Danks and Haynes 2001: 54). Two formal institutions were set up to promote agency-citizen collaboration in forest management: provincial advisory committees (PACs) and adaptive management areas (AMAs). An enhanced collaborative approach to forest management was expected to improve relations between agencies and the public and to reduce conflict over forest management.

In this chapter, I synthesize the literature describing the management and effectiveness of AMAs and PACs during the first decade of the Plan. The documents reviewed use various approaches to evaluate progress, ranging from interviews with agency officials to statistically based survey samples of local community residents. I do not attempt to evaluate these findings based on their technical or scientific merit, but simply to summarize them as they describe the effectiveness of the Plan in enhancing collaboration between agencies and communities.

Monitoring Questions

1. How effective have new forms of collaboration been in engaging local communities?
2. How much has collaboration with the public contributed to achieving the other objectives of the new collaborative mechanisms, such as effective resource management?
3. How effective have the new forms of collaboration been in providing socioeconomic benefits to local communities?

Adaptive Management Areas

The Plan recognizes the critical role played by innovation and experimentation in successful adaptive management. In response, the record of decision (ROD) designated 10 AMAs "intended to provide a geographic focus for innovation and experimentation with the intent that such

experience be widely shared" (USDA and USDI 1994: D-3). The AMAs comprise 1.5 million acres, about 6 percent of the Plan area. Individual AMAs range in size from 92,000 to almost 500,000 acres (table 1-1). Several factors were considered in selecting AMA locations (fig. 1-1):

- Minimizing risk to achieving the conservation objectives of the Plan.
- Providing a mix of public and private lands, to provide opportunities for various owners to cooperate in land management.
- Proximity to communities subject to adverse economic effects from reduced federal timber harvest.

Expectations

The matrix land (land not set aside for reserves or other special designations) allocation and some AMAs were expected to be actively managed to produce the sustained supply of timber expected under the Plan. Local AMA resource managers and communities were expected to use their combined experience and ingenuity to identify approaches that would achieve the conservation objectives of the Plan, without adhering rigidly to all of its standards and guidelines. Primary technical objectives were to develop and evaluate monitoring programs and innovative management practices integrating ecological and economic values. Specific forest management topics to be explored were identified for each AMA. They ranged in emphasis from intensive timber production (Little River AMA) to single-species management (North Coast AMA) to partnerships with state and private land managers (Olympic and Snoqualmie Pass AMAs) (table 1-1).

Adaptive management areas were "intended to be prototypes of how forest communities might be sustained" (USDA and USDI 1994: D-4). Land management and regulatory agencies were expected to collaborate with other government entities, nongovernmental organizations, local groups, landowners, communities, and citizens to achieve these goals. The ROD identifies communities associated with each AMA (table 1-1).

The ROD stipulated several management elements involving collaboration between AMA managers and the public. Each area was to develop a shared, collaborative

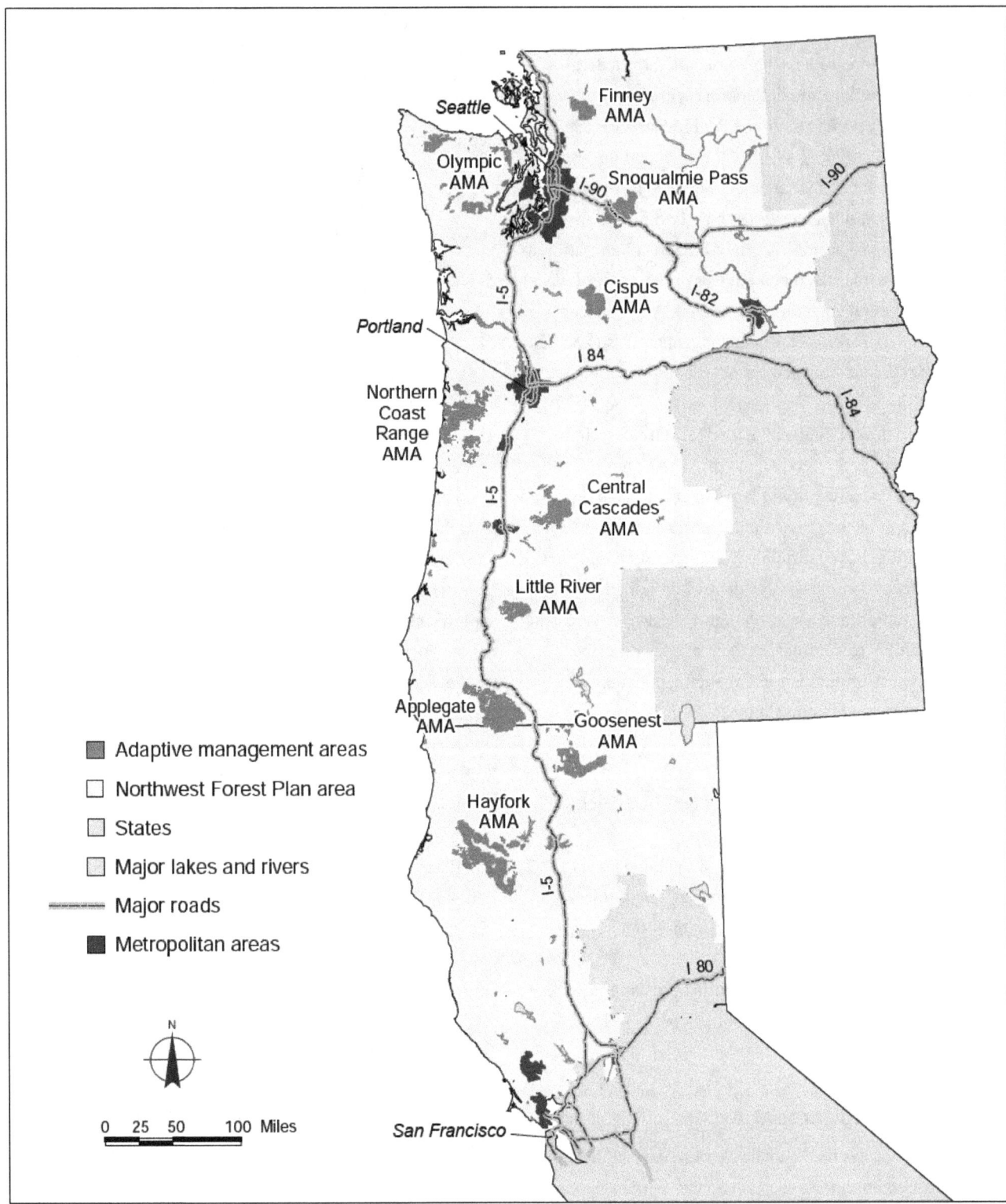

Figure 1-1—Adaptive management areas under the Plan.

Table 1-1—Key characteristics of the Plan's adaptive management areas

State	Name	Size	Ownership	Associated communities	Research and development emphasis
		Acres			
Washington	Cispus	143,900	USFS	Randle, Packwood, Morton	Timber production and forest management
	Finney	98,400	USFS	Darrington	Late-successional and riparian habitat
	Olympic	150,400	USFS	Various counties	Partnership with Olympic State Forest
	Snoqualmie Pass	212,700	USFS, Plum Creek Timber Company, other private, state	Cle Elum, Roslyn	Forest planning on "checkerboard" lands
Oregon	Applegate	277,500	BLM, USFS	Grants Pass, Medford	Forest management
	Central Cascades	155,700	USFS, BLM	Eugene, Sweet Home	Ecosystem landscape processes and forest management
	Little River	91,800	USFS, BLM	Roseburg, Myrtle Creek	Intensive timber production
	Northern Coast	250,000	USFS, BLM	Tillamook, Willamina, Grand Ronde	Marbled murrelet management
California	Goosenest	172,900	USFS	Yreka, Montague, Dorris, Hornbrook	Ecosystem management, commercial timber production
	Hayfork	488,500	USFS, BLM	Hayfork	Forest and ecosystem-management, commercial timber production

vision for the area, knowledge sufficient to meet operating objectives, an operating strategy, and a plan to educate participants and stakeholders. Managers of each area were to define communities to be included in the collaboration; community resources and partners capable of advancing ideas for management; mechanisms for coordinating with local communities; a funding plan; and a plan for integrating community objectives with agency objectives (Pipkin 1998: 31).

The Plan recognized that developing innovative approaches would require communities to have sufficient political capacity, economic resources, and technical expertise to become full partners in the effort. Management also needed to be coordinated across ownership boundaries. Active management of each AMA was to begin with the collaborative development of an assessment and a plan for the area.

In addition to local land managers and communities, AMA operation was to include a third set of parties: agency scientists. Agency researchers were to design experiments testing techniques to meet AMA management objectives under the more flexible direction provided for the areas without compromising the Plan's conservation objectives.

Results and Discussion

Shindler et al. (1996) studied community attitudes related to the Central Cascades AMA only months after the Plan was signed. The researchers based their work on the premise that developing a community-oriented approach for AMAs required an understanding of the degree to which members of associated communities shared preferences for AMA management. The authors conducted opinion research among 744 members of three communities close to the AMA. They identified two community factors that correlated with divergent opinions about AMA management: community dependence on the timber industry and the proportion of retirees among the local population. Two other factors, length of residence and income, did not affect responses.

The authors found that more than 90 percent of community members considered themselves aware of resource management issues. Forty-eight percent felt informed about the Plan. Respondents were supportive of the concept of adaptive management, believing that forest management was best conducted by land and resource agencies in concert with researchers and local citizens. Most respondents in each community supported science and experimentation on selected federal lands. Respondents, particularly those in the nontimber community, believed that federal resource management required significant change, and that AMAs were a generally responsible approach. Note that, although Shindler et al. found that local communities supported the **concept** of adaptive management, a contemporary study (Povey and Synder 1995) found that only 16 percent of local community members were aware of the existence of the Central Cascades AMA.

Timber and nontimber communities were divided over whether the survival of timber workers should be the most important goal of AMAs. Most respondents supported citizen participation, even if it increased government costs. Residents believed that land-management and regulatory agencies, along with local residents and stakeholders, were more fit to influence federal forest management than outsiders.

Shindler et al. concluded that community members would support agencies taking a lead role in AMA management, as long as local residents' input was taken into account. In resource-dependent communities, successful collaboration would be more challenging because these community members believed that agencies were not open to public feedback. The AMA managers would need to overcome lack of trust among local and outside groups. Successful collaboration would require lead agencies to unify constituent groups. If the agencies were unsuccessful, local communities would be reluctant to relinquish control, either to the agencies or to other groups. Continuing community support would be contingent on successful implementation. The authors hypothesized that, should adaptive management

fail to produce better agency decisions, public support for adaptive management might soon fail.

In assembling their report to Congress, Tuchmann et al. (1996) requested information from each Plan-area land management and regulatory agency's regional and field offices. Followup meetings were held with staff and line officers in 30 offices among five agencies. The group found that, by 1995, all AMAs had implemented public-private collaborative activities. Although AMAs differed in amount of activity, several partnerships had been formed with school districts, counties, and local institutions. The team observed a strong appreciation of the value of consensus-building efforts among both agency staff and community members. Compliance with the 1972 Federal Advisory Committee Act (FACA), however, had significantly slowed collaborative efforts: the act required federal officials to temporarily withdraw during adjudication and FACA chartering. A lack of clarity in defining the relation between federal and nonfederal landowners in AMAs further dampened collaboration and general effectiveness. The Tuchmann report's compilation of AMA accomplishments indicates that early management efforts were largely dedicated to the significant workload of planning, assessing, and analyzing required by the Plan and other relevant direction (Tuchmann et al. 1996: 118–119).

The Tuchmann team noted various approaches toward collaborative planning. The public did not participate early in some of the AMA planning process as envisioned in the ROD, but preferred to wait and comment on analyses developed by the agencies. In one AMA, collaboration broke down when the large participatory group polarized. Managers of the AMA went on to work successfully with smaller citizen groups. Managers of another area allowed local community members to lead the initial assessment process. This approach was found to be highly successful.

By the time of the Tuchmann team's assessment, a lack of flexibility under the Plan's standards and guidelines had emerged as a critical factor that limited implementing activities within AMAs. The ability of managers to innovate and experiment was accordingly circumscribed. Regulatory and land management agencies adhered to differing views about the degree of experimentation appropriate within Plan guidance. Nor did operating budgets support rapidly implementing projects as was envisioned in the Plan. Instead, other programs increasingly took priority (Tuchmann et al. 1996: 121).

Stankey and Shindler (1997) examined the establishment of AMAs, proposed a framework for evaluating progress, and identified keys to successful implementation. They noted that agency and nonagency personnel had been disappointed in the apparent inability of the AMAs to attain the objectives outlined by the Forest Ecosystem Management Assessment Team (FEMAT 1993) and the ROD. They saw roadblocks in the lack of specific AMA guides and inadequate organizational support. They attributed the relative success of at least one AMA (Applegate) to an effective public coalition of land-management interests that predated the AMA. Adaptive management areas supported by the agencies internally, but lacking effective public recognition and support, were less likely to attain the objectives in the ROD.

Stankey and Shindler (1997) identified several key issues in effective AMA establishment and management: the need for a publicly recognized social meaning to AMA boundaries, a sense of "ownership" among the public and agency managers, the ability to incorporate personal and experiential knowledge into planning and management, the need to acknowledge diverse viewpoints, and the need for institutional support for rigor in following sound scientific criteria. They noted the ongoing constraint posed by FACA in implementing collaborative management as envisioned by FEMAT and the ROD and suggested restructuring the legislation to address the problem.

They further noted that vague goals and management parameters are impediments to success: clarity is needed in developing AMA purpose and direction. They pointed out that it may be necessary to develop local community capacity to participate in such an undertaking. Finally, they maintained that the issues of inequitable distribution of power and distrust among participants must be faced.

In developing his report to the Plan's Interagency Steering Committee, Pipkin (1998) collected a variety of materials from several sources and interviewed about 75 agency personnel. He found that, although seven AMA

plans had been developed and submitted to a regional work group, work across the AMAs continued to lag behind the expectations set forth in the ROD.

Stankey et al. (2003) provided the most recent assessment of progress. The team conducted an extensive literature review; examined organizational plans and reports; and interviewed 50 agency staff, citizens, and academics. The authors considered AMA effectiveness primarily from the viewpoint of scientific experimentation, but did provide some insights into the effectiveness of AMAs as collaborative mechanisms. Like the Tuchmann team, they noted a lack of agency training and support, with the time and budgets available to AMA staff eroding over time. They described a risk-averse culture in the land management agencies and inflexibility on the part of the regulatory agencies as major impediments. Despite these stumbling blocks, they noted that two AMAs, the Central Cascades AMA and the Northern Coast Range AMA, have succeeded in implementing structured treatments. In their focus on the research aspect of AMAs, the authors noted the need to more fully involve stakeholders as an aspect of gaining social acceptability for designed treatments.

Provincial Advisory Committees

The ROD divided the Plan area into 12 planning provinces (fig. 1-2). For each, the Plan established a PAC to consist of representatives of federal and state agencies, tribes, and others. In actuality, two sets of provincial teams were established to fulfill these objectives. Provincial interagency executive committees (PIECs) for each province are led by the executives of participating national forests and BLM districts and consist solely of agency personnel. Leadership rotates among participating FS and BLM units. Provincial advisory committees are chartered under FACA and consist of up to 29 participants from among a variety of federal, state, county, and tribal governments; the timber industry; environmental groups; recreation and tourism groups; and up to five members at large. This array meets FACA stipulations for representing a broad set of interests while limiting advisory groups to a workable size. The Plan's PACs were formally established under FACA in September 1994.

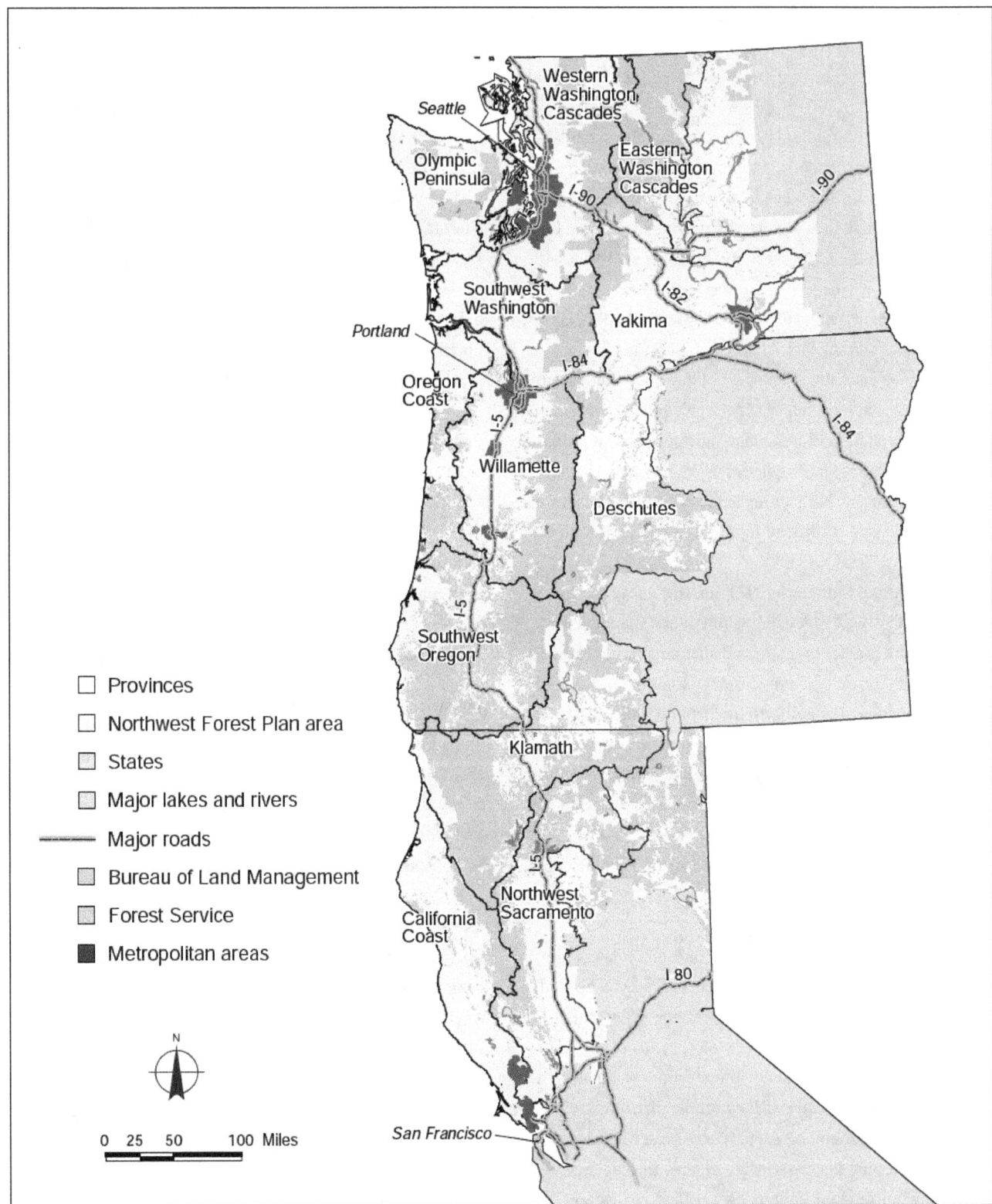

Figure 1-2—Province planning and analysis areas under the Plan.

Expectations

Under the ROD, PACs were to "provide or coordinate analyses at the province level that can provide the basis for amendments to Forest and District Plans and will provide monitoring reports for provinces" (USDA and USDI 1994: E-17). The ROD also directs that PACs are to "encourage and facilitate information exchange and complementary ecosystem management among federal and non-federal partners." The Plan mandates that the Interagency Advisory Committee and Regional Interagency Executive Committee "will continue to develop and refine the appropriate role for these teams at the level of physiographic provinces, Adaptive Management areas, or specific watersheds."

Results and Discussion

The literature summarized here to evaluate PAC effectiveness is limited to two agency reports. Tuchmann et al. (1996) noted early in the period that sometimes PAC chartering under FACA split representation among interests that did not accurately reflect local stakeholders. Provincial advisory committees were seen as redundant with existing bioregional councils. Further, several groups objected to the array of representation required under FACA, contending that the interests of Pacific Northwest communities could more effectively be represented by smaller memberships. In light of PAC boundaries that cross land ownerships, nonfederal PAC participants objected to PAC emphasis on federal land management.

Despite persisting concerns about redundancy, Pipkin (1998) found PACs to be vital to collaboration with state watershed councils and biodiversity councils. Pipkin also found PACs to be effective in enhancing communication between federal agencies and other stakeholders. He further noted that PAC members conduct project-scale compliance monitoring under the Plan. In this monitoring capacity, PACs have met the expectations in the ROD.

Pipkin also noted, however, the lack of a mechanism for communicating between the PACs and the region as envisioned in the ROD, foregoing opportunities for strengthening regional-local ties, for providing regional guidance when necessary, or for facilitating PAC input into larger scale decisions. He pointed out that PACs have not participated in the kind of province-scale analysis foreseen in the ROD as contributing a "basis for Forest and District plans." This work was expected to be central to the mission of the PACs. Lacking commitment to this objective, and without regional guidance or responsiveness, other work of PACs has responded to local projects, participant agendas, and member interests. Committee activities have included education, identifying restoration projects, and reviewing management activities. In some cases, PACs have served to facilitate information exchange between federal and nonfederal initiatives in the province. Members frequently discuss the socioeconomic effects of Plan implementation. Pipkin found that PAC participants generally want stronger links between their committees and regional agency staff. Interestingly, although he found that Bureau of Land Management personnel also want such strengthened ties, Forest Service personnel cite no need for further guidance until requested by the PAC.

Conclusions

How effective have new forms of collaboration been in engaging local communities? How much has collaboration with the public contributed to achieving the other objectives of the new collaborative mechanisms, such as effective resource management? How effective have the new forms of collaboration been in providing socioeconomic benefits to local communities?

Adaptive management areas represent a significant agency investment in collaborative innovation, comprising 6 percent of the Plan area in subregions known to be socially and economically affected by declining timber harvests. Further, they are one of only two land allocations in which sustained timber harvest is expected. Immediately after the signing of the Plan, the work of Shindler et al. (1996) showed that at least some local communities were supportive of collaborative adaptive management. Despite these conditions, the literature shows that in their first decade, most AMAs failed to meet the Plan's expectations.

Initial collaboration with local communities showed promise. The potential for success was diminished early in the period, however, when adjudication and the FACA chartering process forced federal participants to temporarily withdraw, severely affecting local trust in this new form of collaboration. Conflict among some polarized interests also caused collaboration to collapse, forcing federal officials to work with disparate groups rather than in a unified partnership.

Internal agency issues further impaired the ability of AMA managers to collaborate meaningfully. These included a lack of demonstrated, long-term agency commitment to AMA staffing and funding; a lack of incentives to guide and support local AMA managers in shouldering risk; and an unwillingness or inability among the regulatory agencies to consider localized adaptive management—and its potential for small-scale experimental failures—as a legitimate approach for improving larger scale conservation knowledge and techniques (Stankey et al. 2003, Tuchmann et al. 1996).

Given these failures, the collaborative synergy envisioned in the ROD has not materialized among AMAs. Coordination with the public has not been sufficient to leverage the land management agencies' limited willingness and ability to experiment. Few AMAs appear to have gone beyond "business as usual" under the land allocations and standards imposed by the Plan. Accordingly, AMAs have provided little socioeconomic benefit to local communities beyond the other provisions in the Plan.

Despite the cumbersome membership requirements also imposed on them by FACA, PACs have been more successful in engaging local communities. Because of this success, the Plan's PACs were rechartered in 2003 and continue to operate. The PACs have provided a forum for ongoing, multiparty discussion of forest management issues among decisionmakers and local stakeholders. In this capacity, they represent an important step forward over project "scoping" as defined under the 1969 National Environmental Policy Act (NEPA). They have also been successful in completing regionwide, multiparty compliance monitoring. Provincial advisory committee monitoring efforts have fulfilled requirements for implementation monitoring under the Plan. In their monitoring capacity, the Plan's PACs can serve as a basis for future efforts.

But PACs have not delivered the full breadth or positive effects of participatory opportunities envisioned under the Plan. They have not coordinated province-scale analysis to serve as a basis for forest and district plans. Nor does the available literature indicate support from the regional level in developing and supporting a role for PACs in this respect, or in developing an appropriate role related to AMAs. Although PACs have served to improve the flow of information and learning among province interest groups, there is no indication in the literature that they have significantly shaped decisionmaking or resource management. They have thus been unable to affect the flow of benefits to local communities.

Despite these failings, PACs represent an important interim step in developing new mechanisms for collaboration. Resource advisory committees, or RACs, were established by Congress under the Secure Rural School and Community Self-Determination Act of 2000. The act broadens the scale of subregional mechanisms for collaborative ecosystem management, affecting 700 rural counties in 41 states. Like PACs, RACs are multicounty entities created to improve collaborative relations and provide advice and recommendations to the FS and BLM. They are chartered under FACA, with membership providing for smaller groups while still admitting a range of interests. The 15 members of each RAC are drawn equally from among three groups: organized labor, forest commodity production, and intensive uses; environmental and dispersed uses; and elected officials, tribal representatives, educators, and the public at large.

The RACs review and recommend road maintenance, watershed restoration, hazardous fuel reduction, and other projects proposed by counties and others for funding under Title II of the act, which returns a portion of the act's funding to counties for this purpose. The RACs thus play a more immediate role in shaping ecosystem management decisions and investments than do PACs. Although RACs have been in existence for a relatively short time, early research among three committees (Wilson, n.d.) has found members to be satisfied with collaboration and outcomes among their committees. However, the sunset of the Secure Rural Schools Act in 2006 remains the source of considerable concern among members.

The literature shows that, although neither AMAs nor PACs have been entirely successful to date in meeting Plan expectations for engaging the public in new forms of collaboration, both mechanisms have offered significant collaborative opportunities beyond the gridlock and limited NEPA "scoping" mechanism available in the early 1990s.

Both initiatives have been significantly hampered by FACA restrictions. Although the act was designed to prevent inequitable influence in federal decisionmaking, it has caused significant disruptions, imposed cumbersome membership, and ultimately thrown a chill over federal efforts to participate in the collaborative mechanisms designated by the Plan.

Effective AMA management involves a second factor outside the land management agencies' control: a more open interpretation of conservation requirements among the regulatory agencies (Stankey et al. 2003, Tuchmann et al. 1996). Other factors have been beyond the control of local managers responsible for day-to-day implementation. Whether the land management agencies will revitalize the AMA program remains to be seen. Should the attempt be made, federal officials will need to address the likely erosion of public trust and support engendered by the failings of the program in the Plan's first decade.

Less restricted in their operational scope and with broad and sometimes redundant participation, PACs have been able to function despite obstacles like the lack of regional guidance and support. In collaborating with the public through the Plan's PACs, the land-management agencies have been able to achieve other objectives: improved public-private communication and multiparty compliance monitoring. Despite these collaborative successes, the literature provides little evidence that AMAs or PACs have been effective in enhancing or sustaining flows of socioeconomic benefits from federal forests to local communities.

References

Danks, C.; Haynes, R.W. 2001. Socioeconomic research. In: Haynes, R.W.; Perez, G.E., tech. eds. Northwest Forest Plan research synthesis. Gen. Tech. Rep. PNW-GTR-498. Portland, OR: U.S. Department of Agriculture, Forest Service, Pacific Northwest Research Station: 52–62.

Federal Advisory Committee Act of 1972 [FACA]; Act of October 6, 1972; 86 Stat. 770; 5 U.S.C. Appendix 2.

Forest Ecosystem Management Assessment Team [FEMAT]. 1993. Forest ecosystem management: an ecological, economic, and social assessment. Portland, OR: U.S. Department of Agriculture; U.S. Department of the Interior [and others]. [Irregular pagination].

National Environmental Policy Act of 1969 [NEPA]; 42 U.S.C. 4321 et seq.

Pipkin, J. 1998. The Northwest Plan revisited. http://www.reo.gov/library/reports/NFP_revisited.htm. (January 2005).

Povey, D.; Snyder, J. 1995. McKenzie River corridor household survey final results. University of Oregon community planning workshop. Unpublished report. On file with: George H. Stankey, Forestry Sciences Laboratory, Pacific Northwest Research Station, 3200 SW Jefferson Way, Corvallis, OR 97331.

Secure Rural School and Community Self-Determination (Payments to Counties) Act of 2000; Act of October 30, 2000; 114 Stat. 1608–1628; 16 U.S.C. 5000.

Shindler, B.; Steel, B.; List, P. 1996. Public judgments of adaptive management: a response from forest communities. Journal of Forestry. 94(6): 4–12.

Stankey, G.H.; Bormann, B.T.; Ryan, C. [et al.]. 2003. Adaptive management and the Northwest Forest Plan: rhetoric and reality. Journal of Forestry. 101(1): 40–46.

Stankey, G.H.; Shindler, B. 1997. Adaptive management areas: achieving the promise, avoiding the peril. Gen. Tech. Rep. PNW-GTR-394. Portland, OR: U.S. Department of Agriculture, Forest Service, Pacific Northwest Research Station. 21 p.

Tuchmann, E.T.; Connaughton, K.P.; Freedman, L.E.; Moriwaki, C.B. 1996. The Northwest Forest Plan: a report to the President and Congress. Portland, OR: U.S. Department of Agriculture, Forest Service, Pacific Northwest Research Station. 253 p.

U.S. Department of Agriculture, Forest Service; U.S. Department of the Interior, Bureau of Land Management [USDA and USDI]. 1994. Record of decision for amendments to Forest Service and Bureau of Land Management planning documents within the range of the northern spotted owl. [Place of publication unknown]. 74 p. [plus attachment A: standards and guidelines].

Wilson, L.J. [N.d.]. Decision-making and monitoring in resource advisory committees. Hayfork, CA: Watershed Research and Training Center. 10 p. http://www.cbcrc.org/2003speakerpapers/Lisa%20Wilson%20Paper.pdf. (November 2004).

Chapter 2: Collaboration in Forest Stewardship

Ellen M. Donoghue and Susan Charnley

One of the Northwest Forest Plan (the Plan) goals was to improve relations between federal land management agencies and local communities by promoting collaboration between agencies and communities. The Plan's designers believed that the ability of the agencies to meet the principal goal of the Plan—to provide adequate protection for threatened and endangered species—depended on closer collaboration among state and federal land and wildlife management agencies and on developing better and more diverse communication networks between the agencies and local communities (Tuchmann et al. 1996). This chapter examines how collaborative relations and collaboration in forest stewardship have evolved for the four case-study Forest Service (FS) and Bureau of Land Management (BLM) forests since the Plan was implemented, including changes in collaborating with the 12 case-study communities.

Collaboration in forest stewardship comes in many forms and serves many functions. We discuss several forms of collaboration, but others were beyond the scope of the monitoring project. The primary focus is on understanding the status and changes in collaborative forest stewardship and on the relations between community or locally based groups and the case-study forests. We defined collaboration in forest stewardship as the pooling of ideas, tangible resources (such as information, money, labor), or both by communities of interest or place and federal forest-management agencies, to conduct a forest management activity or solve a forest management problem that neither group can solve by itself (adapted from Gray 1985).

The Plan set up specific institutional arrangements to promote collaboration with governmental and nongovernmental stakeholders in the form of provincial advisory committees and adaptive management areas. The Plan also called for a greater degree of collaboration among federal agencies. We did not conduct case-study assessments on all these forms of collaboration; instead, we decided that narrowing the focus on collaborative forest stewardship would allow us to address changes in one type of collaboration, given that an assessment of all collaborative processes in the context of the Plan was beyond the scope of the monitoring project.

Monitoring Question

Did agency and citizen collaboration in forest stewardship improve under the Plan, and did relations between local communities and agencies improve?

Expectations

Collaborative processes, broadly speaking, were expected to create new ways to involve local governments, tribes, and the public in managing the region's forests, in addition to increasing interagency and intergovernmental coordination (Tuchmann et al. 1996). Interagency cooperation and public participation would reduce conflict over forest management (Tuchmann et al. 1996). The Plan did not have specific expectations related to on-the-ground collaborative forest stewardship activities, outside of adaptive management areas.

Data Analysis

We gathered data to assess collaboration trends from a variety of sources. The BLM district reports and a FS database contained data on volunteers. Much of our discussion on collaborative forest stewardship, however, is based on qualitative data from interviews with community and agency representatives from 4 case-study areas and 12 case-study communities; we synthesized these data for this report.[1] For a copy of our interview guide, see volume III, appendix D. A more detailed discussion of our interview methods is contained in volume III, chapter 8; and volume III, appendix D contains a list of people interviewed.

---

[1] More indepth discussion of interview data can be found in:

Buttolph et al. (in press).

McLain et al. (in press).

Charnley, S.; Dillingham, C.; Stuart, C.; Moseley, C.; Donoghue, E.M. Manuscript in preparation. Northwest Forest Plan—the first 10 years (1994–2003): socioeconomic monitoring of Klamath National Forest and three local communities. On file with: S. Charnley, Forestry Sciences Laboratory, 620 SW Main, Suite 400, Portland, OR 97205.

Kay, W.; Donoghue, E.M.; Charnley, S ; Moseley, C. Manuscript in preparation. Northwest Forest Plan—the first 10 years (1994–2003): socioeconomic monitoring of Mount Hood National Forest and three local communities. On file with: S. Charnley, Forestry Sciences Laboratory, 620 SW Main, Suite 400, Portland, OR 97205.

Results and Discussion

We asked community and agency interviewees how collaboration in forest stewardship has changed under the Plan and whether relations between federal land management agencies and local communities was improving. We also asked interviewees to describe the types of collaborative projects they were familiar with and the factors promoting or discouraging collaboration in forest stewardship. Interviewees interpreted collaboration diversely, ranging from volunteer activities contributing to forest stewardship, to agencies listening to the concerns expressed by members of a community. We tried to keep the focus of the interviews on types of collaborations leading to on-the-ground forest stewardship or those indirectly contributing to forest stewardship, such as environmental education.

Types of Collaboration in Forest Stewardship

Collaboration in forest stewardship in the case-study forests had many forms and served many functions. Various governing groups—tribes, state, and local governments—together with forest management agencies, are pooling resources—like time, labor, finances, and ideas—to achieve mutually held forest management objectives. And there are also nongovernmental groups that may be locally, regionally, or even nationally based, such as watershed councils, environmental organizations, economic development groups, and nature or recreation clubs and associations. Individual and corporate landowners also collaborate, as do informal groups, people from a variety of places who work in concert on a particular project, such as a bird or fish count. Some participants are paid or sponsored by their respective organizations to participate in the collaborative activities, but many people volunteer their time or contribute some type of in-kind contribution. Indeed, volunteerism has been, and continues to be, an important way to achieve forest stewardship objectives on the case-study forests.

Most forest stewardship collaboratives described by forest and community interviewees related to recreation, wildlife and fisheries conservation, and habitat protection. Environmental education and community development collaboratives were also mentioned. Because of the less-direct connection to on-the-ground forest stewardship and insufficient data, however, we will not speak specifically of trends in these types of collaboratives. Community and agency interviewees on each of the case-study forests described collaborative projects between agencies and tribes, such as restoring habitat and managing forest products. Collaborative fisheries projects were also mentioned on each forest. Interviewees associated with the Olympic, Mount Hood, and Coos Bay District case studies described a variety of collaborative projects in recreation management, but on the Klamath National Forest, ecological restoration projects were the most commonly mentioned collaborative activities. Recreation collaboratives were diverse in their form and function, including projects involving equestrian associations working on trails or hiking clubs conducting wilderness-use education.

In conducting the community case studies, we purposefully selected community interviewees who represented a range of perspectives in order to address many dimensions of forest management and socioeconomic change (app.). Among this diversity of perspectives, we found that active participation in collaborative forest stewardship by interviewees of the case-study communities was minimal, with some exceptions. Although a focused evaluation of collaboration from the perspective of people engaged in collaborative projects was beyond the scope of the monitoring project, a general assessment of how stakeholders perceived opportunities for collaborative stewardship was possible.

Most of the groups that collaborated with case-study forests drew participants from larger cities or metropolitan areas, or people living in communities near public forests, rather than from a specific forest-based community. One exception is the collaboration between agencies and tribes that appears to be increasing within the case-study forests. Another exception is that in response to the multiple forces that affected the wood products industry since the early 1980s, the Coos Bay District invested heavily in its recreation program in an effort to help local communities build a nature-based recreation and tourism industry on the central Oregon coast. And the interdependency resulting from the patchwork ownership of lands around the Coos Bay District may have encouraged collaboration.

General Trends in Collaborative Forest Stewardship

Most agency interviewees on the case-study forests indicated several ways that collaboration in forest stewardship has changed since the late 1980s. Olympic National Forest interviewees felt that the forest was engaging in more collaborative stewardship activities with the public than in the past. Some, however, felt that collaboration had not necessarily increased, but that the people with whom the forest was collaborating had changed from timber-industry interests to recreation, fish and wildlife, and watershed-oriented interests. Collaborative efforts on the Olympic National Forest have been important to leveraging funds for projects, getting projects accomplished through volunteer efforts, and building long-term relations between the forest and various forest stakeholders and communities.

Over the past decade, the Mount Hood National Forest has increased the emphasis on the use of partners and collaboration to administer forest policy, goods, and services. Interviewees there suggested that this management approach is quite different from the approach and outlook of a decade or more ago. The perception is that then forest managers not only felt they could do the work themselves, but they also tended to prefer to do the work independent of other groups. Currently, partners make up an integral component of forest management on the Mount Hood National Forest. For instance, concessionaires at campgrounds and developed recreation sites (such as Timberline Lodge), outfitters, guides, and volunteers (such as Mazamas wilderness stewards) are increasingly interacting with the public and providing information about forest and recreation management rules, practices, and opportunities. They are also helping conduct on-the-ground forest stewardship activities. Many agency interviewees commented on the high emphasis that the current forest leadership places on collaborative processes.

Compared to the neighboring national forests, the Coos Bay BLM District invested more into direct collaboration with a variety of community partners in the period immediately after the Plan was adopted. One explanation may be that the Coos Bay District had the ability to participate more intensively in collaborative partnerships, particularly during the mid-1990s, because its funding and staffing remained relatively constant, while the need for timber-sale design and implementation dropped precipitously.

Interviewees on the Klamath National Forest noted an increased emphasis on collaboration between the forest and other federal and state regulatory agencies since the Plan was implemented. This emphasis has meant that forest employees in upper management have spent much time, effort, and money working with other agencies on issues relating to resource protection. Some interviewees suggested that the time investment required for interacting with other agencies has taken away from the ability of the forest to interact collaboratively with local communities. The drops in forest budgets and staffing have motivated the forest to develop partnerships with other organized groups such as Ducks Unlimited and the Rocky Mountain Elk Foundation to get work done on the ground. Collaboration through grants and agreements helps the forest leverage resources to get work done, make community members more aware of forest management issues, involve local residents in forest stewardship, and provide local jobs.

The Plan and Collaborative Forest Stewardship

Collaboration in forest stewardship is likely influenced by a host of factors and not by a single one, such as a regional change in forest policy. Nonetheless, to the extent that we are able, we discuss the direct and indirect ways that the Plan has influenced changes in collaborative forest stewardship on the case-study forests.

Ecosystem orientation of the Plan—
The ecosystem orientation of the Plan—and because ecosystems cross boundaries—has broadened the range of forest stakeholders who have interests in, and concerns about, forests and forest management. This expansion of interests has diversified the types of organizations that work collaboratively with the forests. For instance, interviewees on the Mount Hood noted that more than a decade ago the forest was mostly concerned about resource management within the boundaries of the forest and that they worked with a fairly narrow group of stakeholders. Now, a diverse

range of partners, including clubs, local landowners, businesses, and concessionaires collaborate with the forests on on-the-ground stewardship activities across ownerships. Coos Bay District employees indicated that the emphasis on watershed restoration and the need to conduct activities simultaneously on private and federal lands has expanded the use of partnership agreements to get work done.

Interviewees on the case-study forests, particularly the Olympic and Klamath National Forests, report that they have been increasingly working with stakeholders with specific environmental and conservation objectives. Some of these environmental groups acknowledge, and are pleased by, their increased participation in forest stewardship. Yet they remain cautious about whether such relations and commitments by the forests will endure with changes in forest policy. Also, interagency and multiparty collaborations directed under the Plan, such as in provincial advisory committees (see Volume IV, chapter 1), appear to have helped bring new stakeholders to collaborative processes and build relations at watershed, multiownership, and agency-to-agency scales. The extent to which these new forums have delivered benefits to local communities and increased collaborative forest stewardship is unclear, however.

Effects of lower harvest rates and decreased budgets and staff—

Lower harvest rates and the resulting lower budgets and staff, which have both direct and indirect ties to the Plan, have influenced trends in collaboration in two key yet paradoxical ways. With decreasing human and financial resources for forest management activities, the forests have expanded and developed partnerships with groups that shared similar resource management goals. Many agency interviewees suggested that collaborating with like-minded groups was spurred on by the necessity to get the work done. Collaboration and partnerships have become a new way of doing business. For example, the increasing demand for recreation uses and opportunities on the Mount Hood National Forest has not been met with an increasing budget for recreation, which has remained relatively flat (decreasing in real dollars) over the past decade. The contribution of the recreation budget to overhead costs, however, has

increased as other large programs, namely timber, have declined. Thus, managers have turned to numerous partners to help implement recreation management and recreation policy on the forest.

The paradox is that, as budget declines serve as an incentive for innovation and expansion of collaborative processes to achieve forest stewardship objectives, they simultaneously constrain and potentially jeopardize collaborative efforts. Agency interviewees expressed concern that reducing staff and resources has made managing collaborative processes more difficult. Many interviewees spoke of the importance of building relations, but they acknowledged that time—a key ingredient—was growing increasingly scarce with increased workloads and the emergence of more collaboratives. Some agency interviewees were concerned that the forests may not be able to live up to their commitments and obligations in collaborative processes and risk losing the trust of their partners. Case-study FS interviewees also reported that the forests were unable to anticipate the direct and indirect effects of the decreasing timber program on other programs, such as roads, recreation, and volunteer programs, and opportunities for collaboration were initially constrained by these effects.

Agency and community relations—

Although the Plan's emphasis on interagency collaboration and public participation is evident in the increase in multiparty groups, such as the advisory committees and watershed groups, the goal to improve communication and relations with local communities has been less realized. Indeed, some community interviewees felt that the investment in agency-to-agency processes has reduced the emphasis on working with local communities on local issues. Also, they mention a sense that relations have improved and collaborative opportunities have expanded for groups and organizations with interests similar to those of the forests: recreation, watershed, and conservation. Relations have expanded for groups with complementary interests, including youth employment and educational groups that view working in the woods as a way for people to build knowledge and skills, while receiving a wage, course credit, or other benefits. Often these groups are not place-based groups situated in local communities.

The increased diversity of stakeholders and collaborative opportunities on the forest has coincided with a decrease in communication and collaboration with a once-prominent forest stakeholder group, namely the timber community. Traditional ties to communities with previously strong timber orientations have been largely severed. Attempts to build relations in these communities and to find common interests and opportunities in forest stewardship were few in the case-study communities, according to both community and agency interviewees. Broad-based community partnerships have been difficult to establish in the more traditional areas of forest management, such as road construction and maintenance and timber management. And interviewees still working in the timber industry said that the federal forests are no longer key players in timber management. In some places, a notable tension over the inability of the forests to provide a reliable supply of timber may be impeding the creation of collaborative opportunities in forest stewardship with former timber stakeholders.

At the time of the Plan, some communities were more economically diverse than others, or they were beginning to orient themselves toward the forest in new ways, such as with recreation. Some case-study communities had not had strong timber orientations for several years; collaboration in recreation management, in particular, was more evident in these communities than in timber-oriented ones. But, for the most part, the reduction in traditional connections that local communities had to timber management has not been met by comparable increases in connections to the forests through other aspects like recreation or restoration.

Agency interviewees acknowledge multiple benefits of working collaboratively: including getting work done, building relations with the public, and building a sense of civic ownership in the public forests. But these benefits may be difficult to realize in communities without strong connections to the forest. And, they are concerned that a cycle of continued disengagement might follow. Community interviewees pointed out that although some forest employees, most notably some district rangers, were active and involved in the community, this involvement had not translated into collaborative stewardship activities. Many

community interviewees expressed appreciation for, and saw value in, the sharing of information about forest management. Residents, however, often did not see a strong relation between their concerns and forest management. This view, combined with diminished agency presence on the forests—in particular the Forest Service presence—and the decline of timber management activities have created a sentiment in some communities that little mutual interest in collaborative stewardship activities is visible. Although mitigation efforts, such as the Northwest Economic Adjustment Initiative, provided economic development benefits to some communities around the case-study forests, the role of, and contribution by, the forests into these efforts were not widely publicized locally. Thus, opportunities to build or mend relations and connections through mitigation efforts were not fully realized.

A perception among community interviewees is that the Plan has shifted decisionmaking authority from the local forests to the regional and national scale. Some people felt that for this reason collaborative processes would not lead to timely action, and thus participation in such efforts was not worthwhile. Other interviewees noted that many people in the communities are struggling economically and did not have time to get involved in collaborative processes.

Collaboration with tribes under the Plan —
Determining how changes in collaboration between the case-study forests and neighboring tribes relate to the Plan is difficult, given the many factors that may have influenced change. In recent years, recognition by federal and state resource management agencies of tribal rights and the unique relations that tribes have with the United States government has increased (Lesko and Thakali 2001). Appreciation of the formal dialogue and engagement processes with tribes has apparently increased, as mandated in a number of federal acts, including the National Environmental Protection Act of 1970, the National Historic Preservation Act of 1966 (amended 1992), and the Native American Graves Protection and Repatriation Act of 1990. Also, President Clinton's presidential memorandum of 1994 (Clinton 1994) and executive order of 2000 (Clinton 2000) directed all U.S.

agencies to build effective processes for government-to-government relations with American Indian tribal governments. Other factors, such as increased emphasis on protecting anadromous fish habitat of cultural importance to tribes, recent land transfers, and memoranda of understanding between tribes and resource management agencies, have influenced collaborative processes in recent years. Nonetheless, the Plan's emphasis on ecosystems, watersheds, and species protection, coupled with the emphasis on inter-agency and multiparty collaboration, has likely contributed to, rather than detracted from, collaborative processes between most tribes near the FS and BLM case studies.

Interviewees on the Olympic National Forest reported that collaboration between the Quinault Indian Nation and the forest has been high for the past decade. The Plan's emphasis on watershed assessments has prompted interaction and collaboration. In addition, a recent land transfer and the sharing of revenues generated from another parcel of land have produced legal and administrative ties between the agency and the Quinault Indian Nation that continue to fuel collaborative relations.

In 2003, Karuk tribal officials reported that the tribe had established a working relationship with the Klamath National Forest under the Plan and had attempted to implement a number of collaborative projects with the forest. The limitations imposed by the Plan's survey-and-manage procedures had derailed some of these. In addition, the Karuk perceived other roadblocks, including a lack of coordination between the Plan and the Northwest Economic Adjustment Initiative; a lack of collaborative support among some individuals in the Forest Service; and a lack of agency support for the Plan itself. Despite the notable contributions of some individuals in the Forest Service, the situation led to disillusionment among tribe members regarding the willingness of the forest to collaborate with them. In 2003 the Karuk leadership remained interested in actively engaging the Klamath National Forest in collaborative management, but they felt they had been excluded both from providing input and from exercising their traditional knowledge.

Relations with the Coquille Tribe and the Coos Bay District have reportedly improved dramatically since the late 1990s, compared to how they were in the early 1990s. And BLM employees note that they collaborate closely with the Coquille Tribe and the Confederated Tribes of the Coos, Lower Umpqua, and Siuslaw.

Over the past decade, protecting anadromous fish habitat has been an area of increased collaboration among the Confederated Tribes of the Warm Springs and the Mount Hood National Forest, as well as other state and federal agencies and nongovernmental entities.

Volunteerism

Volunteerism is a type of collaboration in which the pooling of interests, resources, and labor often results in on-the-ground forest stewardship activities. But, direct ties between the Plan and changes in volunteerism are difficult to make. Changes in budgets and staffing that coincided with the Plan, however, coupled with the ecosystem orientation of the Plan, have affected volunteer programs on the case-study forests. To assess changes in volunteerism, we combined agency data on volunteers with interview data from the case-study forests. Painting an accurate quantitative picture of trends in volunteerism is difficult, given limitations of, and changes in, methods for collecting and reporting data over the years. We compiled quantitative data for the FS case-study forests for the region, although only recent years were available (table 2-1). For the Coos Bay District, we compiled volunteer data for recent years from annual reports provided by the Coos Bay District Office (table 2-2).

Agency interviewees from the case-study forests indicated that the forests depend heavily on volunteers to contribute to forest stewardship activities. Volunteer programs have evolved, however, with most of the case-study forests reporting increased emphasis on hosted volunteer programs in which agency personnel train and coordinate projects with staff of organized groups. These groups, in turn, train and supervise their members in specific volunteer activities on the forests. Budget and staff declines appear to be a key contributor to changes in volunteer programs, particularly on the FS case-study forests. Although some gains in programmatic efficiency through hosted programs are acknowledged, the decline in direct interaction between

Table 2-1—Senior, youth, and volunteer programs, 2000 to 2003[a]

	Senior community service employment program	Hosted	International volunteers	Volunteers	Youth Conservation Corps	Total
Klamath National Forest						
			Person years[b]			
2000	11.66	16.92		6.21	1.56	36.35
2001	6.95	15.23	0.52	7.72	3.14	33.56
2002	4.68	8.62		6.09		19.39
2003		11.92		4.38	1.61	17.91
			Value of work (dollars)			
2000	251,744	287,396		120,258	38,081	697,479
2001	188,168	295,567	9,554	179,107	74,618	747,014
2002	153,524	156,796		149,942	30,867	491,129
2003		151,875		106,249	45,622	303,746
			Number of enrollees			
2000	26	125		128	5	284
2001	20	97	2	55	19	193
2002	18	84		141	5	248
2003		94		237	12	343
Mount Hood National Forest						
			Person years[b]			
2000	5.96	4.55	0.2	12.92	2.39	26.02
2001	5.78	3.85	0.16	14.51	3.09	27.39
2002	5.25	2.99	0.27	11.32	2.71	22.54
2003		3.30		15.99	3.33	22.62
			Value of work (dollars)			
2000	128,003	92,466	4,367	267,803	39,164	531,803
2001	116,488	75,037	3,711	306,539	43,881	545,656
2002	118,125	60,973	7,661	238,155	55,754	480,668
2003		69,116		379,850	46,462	495,428
			Number of enrollees			
2000	11	209	1	915	15	1,151
2001	14	199	1	952	19	1,185
2002	10	182	1	817	21	1,031
2003		175		1,299	20	1,494
Olympic National Forest						
			Person years[b]			
2000		4.69		11.51		16.2
2001	5.90	9.19		9.55		24.64
2002	9.47	14.06		9.62		33.15
2003		13.66		11.66		25.32
			Value of work (dollars)			
2000		75,059		191,523		266,582
2001	96,886	77,986		168,209		343,081
2002	193,716	198,868		168,221		560,805
2003		275,879		213,786		489,665
			Number of enrollees			
2000		67		506		573
2001	22	105		406		533
2002	17	97		331		445
2003		64		138		202

[a] Hosted programs include, but are not limited to, the Student Conservation Association, Northwest Youth Corps, California Department of Corrections, California Conservation Corps, and Greater Avenues for Independence.

[b] Person year is 260 days and equals one full-time equivalent.

Source: Senior, youth, and volunteer FS database. (Monetary data were not adjusted for inflation.)

Table 2-2—Coos Bay District volunteerism, 1996–2002

Year	Number of volunteers	Volunteer hours	Estimated value[a]
	Individuals/groups[b]		*Dollars*
1996			291,858
1997		17,000	262,383
1998[c]		37,600	509,657
1999	68/2[d]	19,204	267,322
2000	37/1	8,600	117,269
2001	40/1	9,600	102,054
2002	33/1	21,000	377,129

[a] Adjusted for inflation; 2003 dollars.

[b] The district tracks volunteer activity carried out by large groups, such as Girl Scouts or Boy Scouts, as group efforts rather than as individual efforts. County prison volunteer hours were not included in these data.

[c] We are unable to explain the unusually high numbers in 1998.

[d] The BLM began counting couples working as camp hosts as one volunteer, rather than two from FY 2000 onward.

Source: U.S. Department of the Interior, Bureau of Land Management, Coos Bay District (1996–2002).

forest employees and citizen volunteers is seen as negative, as is the necessity of having to turn down, or redirect, individual requests to volunteer because of a lack of capacity to coordinate volunteer efforts.

The recreation programs on all forests have consistently provided opportunities for people interested in volunteering as campground hosts, maintaining recreational sites and trails, wilderness education, and presenting interpretive programs and tours at special sites. For instance, the Elanor trail crew on the Olympic National Forest has been a crew of 6 to 10 retirees ranging from 60 to 80 years old. Other programs on the case-study forests—such as the wildlife, fisheries, and botany programs; the soil, water, and air programs; the reforestation and stand development programs; and heritage programs—have used volunteers to assist with inventory, monitoring, restoration, and interpretation. For instance, the heritage program on the Mount Hood National Forest does not have a budget line item for interpretation (except as program management), but relies on volunteers to do a large amount of the heritage work.

Many volunteers come from outside the communities adjacent to the forests. On the Mount Hood National Forest, for instance, most of the volunteers in the recreation program reportedly come from the Portland metropolitan area.

Local residents, particularly those with strong attachments to specific places or events, volunteer in garbage cleanups, bird counts, fish counts, and other annual events on the forest, but not in high numbers. Community interviewees mentioned few examples of volunteerism in collaborative forest stewardship activities on their respective forests. Some interviewees from the Mid-Klamath community in the Klamath National Forest case study indicated that residents were struggling economically and were not in a position to work for free on behalf of the forest. The pool of residents with the capacity and inclination to get involved in civic activities are occupied with community development activities and may not be able to add to their existing civic commitments. The volunteer coordinator on the Coos Bay District, however, reported that about 50 percent of the volunteers are local and that most of the individual volunteers are long-term workers who contribute 80 to 95 percent of the volunteer hours. Agency interviewees on the Mount Hood National Forest and Coos Bay District also point out that county prison inmates have been another source of volunteers.

We encountered some discrepancies between the agency data on volunteers and perceptions from agency interviewees about changes in volunteer programs. Agency interviewees on the Olympic National Forest reported that the number of volunteers fluctuates from year to year, but has been steadily increasing, and it is a healthy volunteer program. The corporate database, however, shows a steady decrease in the number of volunteers in recent years. This difference may be the result of counting people and projects in different ways from year to year. The perception that the volunteer program is growing is probably more relevant because it reflects day-to-day administrative processes.

For several decades, the Mount Hood National Forest has had some of the highest volunteer numbers in the Nation, which has been attributed to its high environmental and recreational amenities and its proximity to a metropolitan population. Volunteer coordinators reported that the peak numbers of volunteers on the forest were in the late 1980s and early 1990s. Corporate data for recent years show increasing numbers of volunteers, yet fluctuations exist in the number of person-years and the dollar value of the work performed between 2000 and 2003. These fluctuations may be a reflection of the evolution of the volunteer program on the forest. Volunteer coordinators indicated that staff and budget declines have reduced the forest's capacity to manage volunteer programs and that the forest cannot meet the demand for individual volunteer opportunities. As a result, some volunteer programs are now emphasizing hosted volunteers, where the forest trains and coordinates with outside groups who then train and supervise groups of volunteers.

According to corporate data, the number of volunteers on the Klamath National Forest has fluctuated, although it has increased between 2000 and 2003. The data suggest that more people are volunteering for shorter periods of time, and that the dollar value of the work performed by volunteers has been decreasing. Interviewees from the forest stated that the volunteer program has remained fairly stable since the Plan was implemented. They also indicated that running volunteer programs takes a commitment of employee time that has become increasingly scarce as forest budgets and employees decline in number.

Although direct comparisons are not possible, data for the Coos Bay District for roughly the same period as the FS database (2000–2002) show that the district experienced an increase in volunteer hours (although it increased to roughly the same peak as in 1999), an increase in the dollar value of the work performed, but variable numbers of enrolled volunteers. The volunteer coordinator suggested that the decline in volunteer hours between 1997 and 2001 was due in part to the BLM's reluctance to use volunteers for surveys of species because of the concern that volunteer-gathered data might not hold up in court. It also may be due to the increase in Jobs-in-the-Woods programs and other professionalized restoration activities that historically may have provided volunteer opportunities.

Challenges to Collaborative Forest Stewardship

Although several positive and innovative aspects of collaborative forest stewardship are working on the case-study forests, challenges still exist. Some have had direct or indirect connection to the Plan. Those, and other challenges not related to the Plan, are summarized below.

Agency interviewees acknowledge multiple benefits of working in collaborative processes, including getting work done, building relations with the public, and building a sense of civic ownership in the national forests. Participation in collaboratives, however, is difficult in the face of increasing workloads and decreasing budgets and staff. Some program managers said they feel they are just getting by with the resources they have to do their program of work, and engaging new partners and expanding the work seems infeasible. Community and agency interviewees indicated that having leadership in collaboratives—in particular, agency representatives with decisionmaking authority—was important to the progress of collaborative groups because it demonstrates commitment and the willingness to act. Some interviewees, most notably on the Coos Bay District, were concerned that participation in collaborative groups had been delegated to technical specialists who lack decision-making authority.

Agency interviewees on all forests noted that leaders and field employees are some of the most enthusiastic supporters of collaborative processes. Nonetheless, several interviewees on the FS case forests noted that internal cultural barriers to collaboration exist, stemming mainly from an enduring attitude that the FS can do the work best by itself. One challenge may be identifying areas where collaborative approaches can achieve high returns, and other areas where more narrow, traditional approaches are appropriate.

With the broadening of forest stakeholders comes the increased likelihood that perspectives on forest management issues will conflict. Throughout the forest case studies, the formation of groups that initially set out to address a management issue or series of issues is evident, but their inability to unify under common forest stewardship objectives has derailed some groups. For instance, community interviewees on the Klamath National Forest, who were involved in a collaborative group that formed at the onset of the Plan, said the group intended to address forest management issues but eventually a few strong dissenting voices led to a stalling of the collaborative process. Although this experience became a disincentive for some members to participate in collaborative processes in forest management, interviewees noted that they could apply knowledge gained through that experience to collaboratives that addressed other, less controversial objectives, such as water and fisheries management.

Conclusions

Did agency and citizen collaboration improve under the Plan, and did relations between local communities and agencies improve? The Plan has had direct and indirect, positive and negative effects on collaborative forest stewardship on the case-study forests and communities. The Plan's ecosystem focus and emphasis on interagency collaboration encouraged interactions among public and private landowners and broadened the range of stakeholders and opportunities for collaborative processes. A variety of groups, together with forest agencies, are pooling resources, such as time, labor, finances, and ideas, to achieve mutually held forest stewardship objectives. Faced with challenges of decreased budgets and staffs, the forests have been able to maintain viable, productive, and multibeneficial collaborative projects and programs. The volunteer programs are good examples of programs that are evolving and seeking

new collaborative opportunities in the face of administrative and budgetary constraints.

Increased diversity and innovation in collaboration, however, has coincided with a decrease in communication and collaboration with a once-prominent forest stakeholder, namely the timber community. The disconnect between timber-based communities and forest management and the implication it would have on collaborative relations were unanticipated consequences of the reduction in timber harvests under the Plan. In general, collaborative activities, as reported by community interviewees who represented a diversity of perspectives, were minimal with some exceptions, such as Tribal collaboratives. New connections have yet to replace old timber ties in some communities. Many interviewees from former timber-based communities tended to feel disassociated from, or unaware of, current forest policies and practices or had little direct concern with forest management. And yet, some former timber industry employees who remained in their communities felt that their skills, knowledge, and experience in forest management could serve contemporary forest management practices but were not being used. Other factors that affected the participation of community residents in collaborative resource management, beyond the necessity of a shared mutual interest or stake, included a shortage of residents with skills to do the work, residents with the time to participate, consistent players and participation, organized groups with resources, and residents who are not struggling to make ends meet. We focused on common themes that emerged from the four local cases, and do not know if, and to what extent, the results reported here can be generalized to the Plan area as a whole.

Literature Cited

Buttolph, L.F.; Kay, W.; Charnley, S.; Moseley, C.; Donoghue, E.M. [In press]. Northwest Forest Plan—the first 10 years (1994–2003): socioeconomic monitoring of Olympic National Forest and three local communities. Gen. Tech. Rep. Portland, OR: U.S. Department of Agriculture, Forest Service, Pacific Northwest Research Station.

Clinton, W.J. 1994. (April 29). Executive memorandum on government-to-government relations with Native American tribal governments. Washington, DC: The White House, Office of the Press Secretary.

Clinton, W.J. 2000. (November 6). Executive order 13175—Consultation and coordination with Indian tribal governments. Washington, DC: The White House, Office of the Press Secretary.

Gray, B. 1985. Conditions facilitating interorganizational collaboration. Human Relations. 38: 911–936.

Lesko, L.M.; Thakali, R.G. 2001. Traditional knowledge and tribal partnership on the Kaibab National Forest with an emphasis on the Hopi interagency management. In: Clow, R.L.; Getches, D.H; Sutton, I., eds. Trusteeship in change: toward tribal autonomy in resource management. Boulder: University Press of Colorado: 281–301.

McLain, R.J.; Tobe, L.; Charnley, S.; Moseley, C.; Donoghue, E.M. [In press]. Northwest Forest Plan—the first 10 years (1994–2003): socioeconomic monitoring of Coos Bay district and three local communities. Gen. Tech. Rep. Portland, OR: U.S. Department of Agriculture, Forest Service, Pacific Northwest Research Station.

Tuchmann, E.T.; Connaughton, K.P.; Freedman, L.E.; Moriwaki, C.B. 1996. The Northwest Forest Plan: a report to the President and Congress. Portland, OR: U.S. Department of Agriculture, Forest Service, Pacific Northwest Research Station. 253 p.

U.S. Department of the Interior, Bureau of Land Management. 1996–2002. Annual program summary for the Bureau of Land Management Coos Bay District. North Bend, OR: Bureau of Land Management. http://www.or.blm.gov/coosbay. (August 31, 2004). Annual.

Appendix: Methods and Interview Guide

Methods

Our evaluation of how effective adaptive management areas (AMAs) have been is based on secondary source material. Refer to that material for a discussion of methods used to assess AMAs. Our discussion of how effective Provincial Advisory Committees (PACs) and Resource Advisory Committees (RACs) have been at promoting collaborative forest stewardship is based on both secondary source material and informal discussions with PAC and RAC members, both during and outside of committee meetings.

The analysis of trends in volunteerism and partnerships is based on agency data relating to volunteers and other work programs, as well as partnership agreements (e.g., memoranda of understanding, cooperative agreements, joint venture agreements). To document these trends, we first updated a survey of the many volunteer and partnership databases that exist within the Forest Service to determine how useable they are for monitoring. This survey was begun by the Forest Service Partnership Taskforce. Databases surveyed include infrastructure database (INFRA), Wildlife, Fish and Rare Plants (WFRP), Senior, Youth, Volunteer (SYV), Economic Action Programs (EAP), and National Fire Plan Operations and Reporting System (NFPORS). These databases have not been fully populated with historical data and typically contain only very recent data. They are not linked together and contain redundant and contradictory information. Additional data on trends in collaborative forest stewardship, in particular related to volunteerism, were gathered during case study interviews with forest employees and community representatives and stakeholders.

Once the data sources were located, we queried them for information on our case-study forests. The Mount Hood National Forest served as a pilot test for this exercise, as that forest has an active partnership program. We refined our monitoring methods by using the Mount Hood and then applied them to the rest of the national forests in the plan area.

We wanted to track trends in partnership agreements as part of monitoring collaboration in forest stewardship. However we encountered substantial data problems that prohibited us from conducting an analysis of partnerships within the time and resources available for the project. One of the problems associated with monitoring partnership agreements is that they are removed from the database once they are terminated. Thus, agency databases only contain information on those partnership agreements that are active. This makes it difficult, if not impossible, to obtain data regarding past agreements. Hard copies of these agreements may be stored in Forest Service warehouses, but it was impractical to try to retrieve documents from warehouses for purposes of this monitoring report.

Interview Guide

Purpose: Data gathered in this section should contribute to understanding the evolution, or not, of how and why communities have participated in collaborative forest stewardship with the national forest/BLM since the NWFP. Specific projects and motivations for engaging in such projects that are directly related to the NWFP should be identified. Projects and motivations not directly tied to the NWFP should be described separately in order to arrive at an overall sense of how public engagement and collaborative forest stewardship have changed.

Intro:

I'm interested in how your community, or local groups that you are involved with, collaborates with Forest X in resource management activities on the forest or near the forest. I'm also interested in how overall engagement in collaborative forest stewardship activities between the community, local groups, and Forest X has changed over the past decade. More specifically, I'd like to discuss what types of actual on-the-ground collaborative activities occur. (Researchers: If responses to prior sections indicate that the interviewee is well informed about the NWFP, please include reference to it when asking about change over the past decade. The below questions assume that the interviewee knows little about the components of the NWFP.)

TOPIC: Change in general engagement with FS/BLM

(1) Has your community/group's overall engagement with the National Forest changed over the past ten years? Has it increased, decreased, or stayed the same?

(2) How and why has it evolved or stayed the same?

TOPIC: Change in on-the-ground collaborative forest stewardship

(3) What types of on-the-ground collaborative forest stewardship activities does your community engage in with the Forest/District?

(4) If none, why not?

TOPIC: Objectives and motivations for collaborating

(5) Please describe some of the objectives of those collaborations or partnerships.

(6) What motivates your community/group to collaborate with Forest X? Who usually takes the initiative to establish these collaborations?

TOPIC: Benefits of collaborating

(7) How does the community/group benefit from the collaborations? What have been some of the successes?

(8) Have there been any indirect benefits (such as skills developed, increased networking, improved relations to Forests)?

TOPIC: Barriers to collaborating (community and FS/BLM)

(9) What do you see as the biggest barriers, internal to your community, to collaborating with the National Forest in resource management activities (such as trust levels, community leadership/capacity, community cohesion)?

(10) What do you think are the biggest barriers that the National Forest/BLM has to collaborating with your community (or local communities) in resource management activities (such willingness/availability of forest leadership/staff to collaborate, lack of personnel, lack of funds)?

TOPIC: Future direction of collaboration

(11) Are there any types of collaborative activities that you would like to see developed or expanded? Why?

TOPIC: Plan goal

(12) What progress has been made on meeting the Plan goal to improve relations between federal land management agencies and local communities, and promote collaborative forest management and joint forest stewardship activities?